I0190064

Echoes of the Other Me

Know me through my poems

Advik Ekre

Advik Ekre

Advik Ekre

Dedication

For every type 1 diabetic warrior who, from a tender age, learns to trade simple pleasures yet still greets life with a radiant smile and the families who stand beside them, unwavering.

These poems were my quiet support systems and my channel of expressions. I offer them now, in hope that they bring you the same solace they brought me.

Advik Ekre

List of Poems

Advik Ekre

Advik Ekre

In Memory Of

I lost my maternal grandfather **"Shri Vitthalrao Pidurkar"** when I was 1 year old and lost my paternal grandfather **"Shri. Arunrao Ekre"** when I was 3 years old.

I have always heard stories of their hard work and strong value system from my parents.

I am sure their blessings are always with me and remembering them while publishing my first book of poems.

Advik Ekre

Values Or Dreams?

I faced a substantial divide
Either facing my values with pride
Or letting them go for the quick prize
The contrasting crossroads in my eyes.

I pondered in silence, the choice I must make
To follow my dreams or my values forsake
But wisdom whispered, as stars softly gleam
I chose to reshape the course of my dream.

Advik Ekre

Faithfull Dreams

I told my dreams today, "Go, take some rest
I am tangled in life's trials, not at my best"
But dreams, as my true friend, refused to part
Whispering softly, "We'll stay, close to your heart."

We'll sit outside your eyelashes, just near
Waiting patiently, for when your mind is clear
We find joy and privilege only in your gaze
We'll wait for the moment to enter again.

Kindness of Pain,

Absence of Joy

Words used to be richer expressing my state
No stillness in soul, thoughts shine
Once was a blooming and content mind
Now it has become silent and blind.

Have I found all the joy life can bestow?
So perfect that it has no strife that I know
If joy is gone, or pain grown kind
I wonder what's left for me to find.

Advik Ekre

A Quiet Light Behind Me

Dad,
As I prosper, grow and go forward
I want to pause and look back
To again walk those footsteps, we once shared
So, I can relive our memories on a beautiful path.

For every step I take ahead
Is a step that echoes where you've been
In every stride, your spirit's there
Guiding me with a quiet, steady path to win.

I want to re-live the dreams those together we have
seen
I want to see it again through your eyes, calm and
serene
Your hopes and dreams gleam through people's plight
My goal is to brighten their lives with your illuminating
light.

Advik Ekre

What You Don't See

What you don't see
is pain of my grind
Not some random luck
That you think I find.

My life's like a pearl
Looks shiny and cool
But it took a lot of work
Not just some magic rule.

The oyster? It struggles
It's messy and tough
And that's how I got here
Not by "just enough.

So don't discard the shine
If you don't see the fight
This glow wasn't easy
I earned this light.

Me. Through My Own Eyes

No matter what I do
In their eyes, I'm never enough
They see me small
Like I'm just not tough.

But their reflections don't matter
It's mine that I need to see
When I look in the mirror
I want to be proud of me.

My own true satisfaction
It's not their applause or cheers
It's knowing I stood tall
Even with doubts and fears.

I won't let myself down
Not for their shallow soul
I'll hold my head high
winning them is not my goal.

Advik Ekre

Life Is My Preacher

I didn't learn life with prayers and rules
No one told me "What's right, what's cruel"

I stumbled, I lost, I rose again
The failure taught me along with pain.

My lessons are scars, my book is The Street
Learnt from tough lessons, life feels complete.

The Way, You See Me

When I look into your eyes
I see myself I never knew
in your mind a handsome view
A reflection shaped by you.

For the world I'm not good enough
Maybe my face doesn't fit their frame
a different vision is needed to see through me
Your eyes hold truths they cannot see.

In them, I'm more than their whispers
More than their stares
I'm something real
Something rare.

Let them think what they want to believe
Their words no longer make me grieve
Because your heart has known the real me
One day everyone will see the way you see me.

Advik Ekre

The Calm You Bring

Sometimes mind feels the weight
doubts screaming, racing thoughts
Dreams so close and still so far
crossing the sea to touch horizon.

Questions swirl
Answers hide
I am not even mine
Lost in the noise inside.

Sense prevails with my shadow in your eyes
the chaos softens in their light
It's like the answers were always there
Waiting just to get moment right.

.

I Still Have Hope

I knew something was wrong
A shadow in the distance
But I called it a dream
And left it behind.
I moved on
Telling myself it was nothing.

I saw darkness behind the light
And I thought it was you
Your shadow
I reached for it
Like chasing the horizon
Always there
Never mine.

When you smiled
I thought it was a mirror
A window to your soul
For your dreams
I gave everything.

Advik Ekre

As you have gone away from life
The dreams we built
I'm burning them to ash
But as the flames rise
I hope that I'll see tears in your eyes.

And if those tears fall
I'll catch them
Turn them into pearls
Even after it's all gone
I'd do anything
To make something beautiful

Advik Ekre

I will Stand with You

Not every word needs to be said
Silence is louder when left unsaid
Every breath I have is for you
Every moment to touch your soul.

When you close your eyes at night
Sky full of dreams, bold and bright
The wish you chase, the life you see
Standing with you, you'll always find me.

Advik Ekre

I Have Not Lost Yet

feels everything is falling apart at once
want to fly, but wings don't work anymore
The dreams seem distant too far to touch
I sit in silence, thinking they are beyond reach.

What saves me is my own who stays close
they make me smile, remove thorns from roses
So I hold on, even when it hurts like frost
with hope I'll find what I thought I had lost.

Advik Ekre

Where I Am Found Again

forgetting myself in this endless, tiring game
Chasing a dream that fades just like a flame
Every step forward feels like I'm more lost
Happiness keeps running, but at what cost?

I smile on the outside, but inside I fall
No one hears when I'm screaming through it all
Let me leave the past behind, no memory ever
Let me hide in your heart and stay forever.

Advik Ekre

In the Echo of Us

I wish a day should rise, just me and you
Only your heartbeat breaking through
I would forget the falls, the climbs, difficult plight
If you stayed with me, every day and night.

It feels all gone when you're not by my side
But you show up in dreams where I can't hide
Your voice makes even silent words feel deep
And I search for you in memories I keep.

We've fought storms, difficult ones, side by side
And with each wave, our bond refused to hide
When my mind drowns in a million things unsaid
You live in the echo that never really fled.

So I wish again, a day should rise, just me and you
Only your heartbeat breaking through.

Advik Ekre

My Grandmother

A small old house with priceless worth
That's her whole world full of love and warmth.

She stays so calm when joy is in abundance
And doesn't cry even though pain is persistent.

She won't preach life only with hollow words
She listens deeper than the voice is heard.

No matter what success or awards I earn
She won't cheer loud, just want me to learn.

She doesn't trust joy that fades too fast
She looks for serenity, the kind that lasts.

Hard times came and questioned my existence
But her silent prayers pulled me from remnants.

She's not just a part of where I begin
She's my strength that lives within.

Advik Ekre

When the Storm Learned to Bow

A rangoli boomed outside my small front door
Saffron, Green, Blue, and White on the floor.

When they come together, they all had their space
Each color glowing with its own grace

Then one day, a storm came to test
It swirled and howled, disturbing their rest.

Saffron stepped up, said, "Try Green instead
And Green pulled Blue close, full of dread.

Saffron stepped up, said, "Take Green with you"
And Green pulled Blue close, said "Blue Is for you".

But White stood firm, calm like a monk
"You'll not win", spoke to the storm.

"You'll spoil their form, throw them around
But your rage will instead pull you down.

Advik Ekre

"Let me come with you," White gently said
I'll help you shine bright, not just erase.

the storm stood still and thought for a while
Then softened its gust and sparkled with smile.

Now that rangoli still lives on my street
Where colors and calm in harmony meet.

Advik Ekre

Robots, No Blood in Their Smiles

Machines make magic but heart to heart distance seem
so long
Tomorrow we might forget where real souls belong.

We will trade warm hugs for blinking, empty eyes
While love and laughter slowly go away and eventually
die.

Robots speak words but never bleed or cry
Try to teach them love, they'll only lie.

Their hearts are wires, cold under metal skin
No dreams, no fears, no breaking from within.

Every choice they make is numbers in disguise
They wear a smile, but it's a mask of lies.

And when their perfect minds all crash and burn
There will be no second chance, no way to return.

Advik Ekre

Whispers After I'm Gone

At some point, my name may fade in the air
Wind may lose color, love still holding prayer.

Faith will still whisper, but rage will lose fight
Words will stay silent, but roar in the night.

I may be there, or maybe just a dream
But you'll remember my fire, my furious scream.

The roads I carved in lost, forgotten lands
Try everything to hold but will flow like sand.

Just Open Your Eyes

You don't need a revolution to heal this land
Just open your eyes, learn to understand.

You have lived too long in a cold, wired dream
Face the fire now, walk the burning stream.

Advik Ekre

Not the One to Break

Staying busy in studies just hides the hurt and rain
Losing sleep at night just runs from dreams and pain.

I do not know where I started, where I even stand
Got tired, thought I made it — empty in my hand.

But destiny never made a straight road for me
It twisted the end just so I couldn't be free.

For a moment, I felt everything was gone
Dreams crushed, hope dead before the dawn.

I cringed, yeah — but I'm not the one to break
I grabbed my fate, my dreams, my soul to remake.

Stay True

When your dreams are clear, the sky seems clear blue
Clouds may cast shadows but can't break through.

If you stay honest, wisdom prevails, decision will be
wise
But fake yourself once, you'll fall from your own eyes.

Advik Ekre

Away from Virtual Disguise

A flood of facts, but truth feels far away
My heart gets lost in what so many voices say.

Let me fail, learn, not just aimlessly scroll
want to feel your heartbeat, up-close and real.

Pain Chose Me,

But

So Did Purpose

Sometimes I feel why pain chose the simple soul like
mine?
May be strong roots make tree grow strong with time.

Each choice I make feels heavy for my years
I've learned to be happy by holding back my tears.

Maybe God saw a fighter in my eyes
Hence I got not only battles but strength also to rise.

Advik Ekre

True Friends

We need true friends who would fight the world for
you
Not just for laughs, but when you're feeling blue.

If I lose my way, they will show me right path
Walk away from darkness and walk me into light.

Honest heart, same values, not fake or pretend
A real one who stays, right till the end.

We need that friend who sees our silent cries
Who shows up real, not hiding truth with lies.

If I feel weak, they will hold me till I stand
Not just momentary but with a steady hand.

Friend, who shares my flaws and still will not leave
That kind of love is all I need to happily live.

Guided by Blessings, Lit by Hope

I want to keep my sorrows deep inside me
let my joy flow without boundaries and free.

Someone's dream, a fleeting, fragile flame
I want to work hard, to ease their pain.

I gather blessings like stars in quiet skies
They might just guide me when the dark days rise.

Advik Ekre

Safe in the Calm of You

I want to disappear deep inside a part of your soul
My own pain, worries in love, taking a toll.

I used to care what the whole world might say
But your calm eyes make that noise fade away.

Advik Ekre

More Than Just a Name

Everyone says, what's in the name? Just a few letters
Yet somehow it decides who gets love, who gets
stares.

I thought a grandiose name would make me feel tall
But at end my truth stood by me, no name at all.

Advik Ekre

Where I Don't Belong

Everyone looks content overseas, like life's a stage
they already know
Clean roads, tall buildings, perfect smiles in a glow.

Everyone seems so happy, smart, like fate had time
But I turn around, and no heartbeat matches mine.

Advik Ekre

www.ingramcontent.com/pod-product-compliance
Lightning Source LLC
Chambersburg PA
CBHW021142020426
42331CB00005B/863